AN ODE TO SPEED

WHY A FOCUS ON COST MAKES ORGANIZATIONS WEAKER, LESS PROFITABLE, AND LESS COMPETITIVE

JUSTIN ROFF-MARSH

Copyright ©2025 Justin Roff-Marsh

All rights reserved.
No part of this book may be reproduced, stored in a retrieval system, or transmitted by any means, electronic, mechanical, photocopying, recording, or otherwise, without written permission from the copyright holder.

First Edition

ISBN: 9798310490482

www.justinroffmarsh.com
www.ballistix.com

Dedicated to
Warren and Sylvia Roff-Marsh
who instilled in me a love of reading

and

Bo Hye Roff-Marsh
who is always the first to read each page I write

Contents

Introduction 1
   Note: Efficiency is another word for cost reduction 2

Chapter 1
An ode to speed 5

Chapter 2
Cost accounting 7
   "We need cost accounting" 7
   "It's better than the alternative" 8
   "In most situations, it's accurate enough" 9
   The extent of the problem 10

Chapter 3
Cost accounting's fatal flaw: bad math 13
   Profit is probably not what you think it is 13
   The forgetting of time, institutionalized 14
   Ease of use 15

Chapter 4
The direction of the solution 17
   A Rosetta stone 18
   Is this insight useful? 20
   Speed as an antidote to chaos 21

Chapter 5
The solution: Throughput-based reasoning 25
   Two approaches to predictions 25
   A simple, bottom-up approach to management decisions 27
   Containing costs 28

Chapter 6
Two critical value chains 31

Chapter 7
An introduction to metrics 35
    A system of metrics 35

Chapter 8
Retooling for speed 39

Chapter 9
An ode to speed: part 2 41

Chapter 10
Coda: two examples of Throughput-based decision-making 43
    How should a manufacturer of countertops price a new product 43
    The danger of the departmental profit and loss statement 45

Further reading 49

Assistance is available 49

Bonus Content: Double-Digit Growth 51

Introduction 53	Customer Service 73
1954 55	Onboarding 74
1959 57	Engineering 75
The lesson 59	Account Management 77
What could possibly go wrong? 61	And now, to grow! 78
Revenue: four basic truths 63	Sales and Marketing 79
Adrift from reality 67	Look what you've done! 83
The design flaw and how to fix it ... 68	Two loose ends 84
The magic of loose coupling 71	Double-digit growth 87

About the Author 89

Introduction

Imagine you were to take over the management of a Formula One team, and rather than focusing on the car's speed, you focused on reducing fuel consumption.

That would be stupid, right? Idiotic, even!

But this is the orthodox approach to business management. Not surprisingly, the result is that almost every business is weaker, less profitable, and less competitive than it could be.

If yours happens to be one of these businesses, your only saving grace is that your competitors have likely adopted the same management approach.

It's not that managers are unaware of the importance of speed. There are certainly speed-based metrics (on-time delivery performance, inventory turns, and debtors' days, for example). The problem is that these are exceptions, not the rule. The default focus is cost.

This book explains why a focus on cost minimization is harmful to both the profitability and the growth of businesses. It then describes how you can (and why you should) shift your focus to the maximization of speed.

The ideas presented here are derived from Eliyahu Goldratt's Theory of Constraints. If you've ever read his best-selling book (The Goal), much of the reasoning here will be familiar.

NOTE: EFFICIENCY IS ANOTHER WORD FOR COST REDUCTION

You might object to my characterization of cost as the alternative to speed. You might argue that you pursue efficiency, an optimal mix of speed and cost.

In practice, efficiency-improvement initiatives are cost reduction by another name. Economists might measure efficiency at the level of the organization, but managers never do. In practice, efficiency improvement is performed at the level of departments, machines, or even individual contributors.

The goal of efficiency improvement is to ensure that the resource in question is fully activated (always busy). If the resource can't be fully activated because it lacks work or because of a lack of demand for whatever it produces, then the only viable alternative is to downsize (or eliminate it).

Introduction

Chapter 1
AN ODE TO SPEED

If I were asked to give a single piece of advice to the owner of an industrial business (or any business, for that matter), I would say to *increase your organization's clock speed.*

By *clock speed,* I mean the default rate at which work gets done within your organization—not just some work, but all work.

If unnecessary work is being done in your organization, you should eliminate it; however, if it's necessary, it should probably be done faster.

Modern businesses are incredibly complex systems, which is to say, *massively interconnected.* If a department anywhere within your organization performs important but non-urgent activities at a less-than-optimal rate, it's almost certainly causing drag somewhere that really matters.

And if you have a department anywhere within your organization that is not marching to a time-based metric, that department is *definitely* operating at a less-than-optimal rate.

But, if your organization is typical, most departments march to cost- rather than time-based metrics, which brings us face to face with the villain in our little story.

Chapter 2
COST ACCOUNTING

The villain, of course, is Cost Accounting.

It's widely understood among experienced executives (and accountants) that cost accounting has problems. Most are aware of situations where the cost-based approach to management decision-making yields laughable results.

But the standard response to these problems is basically to shrug. "We need cost accounting. It's better than the alternative. In most situations, it's accurate enough."

The first two of these responses are correct. The third is wrong. So, let's take a look at each briefly. And then, let's explore the core problem with cost accounting and an alternative approach to management decision-making.

"We need cost accounting"

It's true that organizations need cost accounting. It's critical for reporting the organization's historical performance to external stakeholders (particularly shareholders and various statutory authorities).

So, where financial accounting is concerned, cost accounting is here to stay. And that's fine because the problems inherent in cost accounting do not raise their ugly little heads in the generation of (historical) reports.

But we're not here to talk about reporting. We're here to talk about management decision-making. And that's a forward-looking activity. No law dictates that cost accounting be used for management decision-making.

Organizations do this because they lack a practical alternative (and because everyone else does it!).

"It's better than the alternative"

Remember when you were first exposed to business? Perhaps you were a new hire at a big, scary corporation. I guess there was a point where you suggested that the organization do something because it would make a bunch of money, and you were chided for not considering all the *hidden costs* associated with your proposition.

Maybe a customer asked to make a bulk purchase at a lower price, and you got excited about the juicy margin that would land in the corporate bank account. Then, a more seasoned executive pointed out that the "real" cost of filling that order was much more than you realized because you needed to allocate a portion of the organization's operating expenses to calculate the "profit" in the deal.

This hypothetical highlights both the default alternative to cost accounting (which is to ignore operating costs altogether) as well as the solution provided by cost accounting (which is to allocate—via some method—some portion of operating costs) to every "profit" calculation.

Given those two alternatives, cost accounting is certainly the preferable one! But it's a terrible mistake to assume that these are the only possible approaches to management decision-making.

"IN MOST SITUATIONS, IT'S ACCURATE ENOUGH"

It's true that cost accounting can yield accurate results in some situations. And it's also true that it can yield laughable results in others.

The distinguishing factor is the predictability of transactional volume.

This is why cost accounting works just fine when reporting on the past. Because the past has already occurred, you have perfect knowledge of the number of transactions in the period under consideration.

But, when considering the future, you're unlikely to have that same level of confidence. Furthermore, many decisions involve proposals that are likely to cause a change in transaction volume.

So, where transaction volume is concerned, cost accounting works well when the organization is in stasis. It can furnish you with dependable answers if you're attempting to make decisions that do not impact the rate at which your customers buy things.

However, if you're contemplating a change that is likely to impact transaction volume, cost accounting is effectively useless as a decision-support system.

It's worth pausing to consider the implications of this. Cost accounting (as it's typically used) provides managers with dependable information only when they consider proposals that will result in them making minimal functional changes to their organizations.

But on the occasions when they are bold enough to propose something that might actually change the way their organizations function, their default decision-support tool punishes them with wildly unpredictable conclusions!

THE EXTENT OF THE PROBLEM

In a moment, I'll explain an obvious problem with the math underpinning cost accounting. And we need to acknowledge that problem before we contemplate a solution.

But it's important to note that lousy math is not the extent of the problem.

The bigger issue is that managers build a mental model of their organizations, and cost accounting is an integral part of this model.

This means that cost-based reasoning is applied by default to day-to-day management decisions, even when no math is involved.

But it gets worse. Because there are frequent situations where cost-based reasoning furnishes managers with obviously false conclusions, managers suffer from regular cognitive dissonance. You might expect this cognitive dissonance would cause managers to challenge their mental model of the organization, but, for the most part, it doesn't. The more common effect is that managers hunker down and become even more defensive of their belief system and even more insistent that others respect the answers furnished by their cost-based reasoning!

Taiichi Ohno, the father of the Toyota Production System, once said: "It was not enough to chase out the cost accountants from the plants. The problem was to chase cost accounting from my people's minds".

Cost Accounting

The Machine is Justin Roff-Marsh's Axiom award-winning book on sales transformation.

Build a ridiculously efficient sales process to out-communicate, outsell and ultimately, outgrow your competition.

SCAN TO BUY

bit.ly/3YFONte

Chapter 3
COST ACCOUNTING'S FATAL FLAW: BAD MATH

It's impossible to understand the bad math that underpins cost accounting without first understanding the concept of "profit".

PROFIT IS PROBABLY NOT WHAT YOU THINK IT IS

If our goal is to have an intelligent conversation about business, it's critical that we understand that profit is not what you get when you subtract raw material costs from revenue: that's *contribution margin*.

Profit is the stuff that a business generates. Profit is an attribute of a business. It is NOT an attribute of a transaction, a customer, a branch office, or even a project. Only businesses generate profits. It makes *absolutely no sense* to talk about a profitable transaction, a profitable customer, a profitable project, or even a profitable division.

Okay, so what is profit?

In simple terms, profit is *cash that is released by a business that can be used by the owners of that business for other things*. It's true that profit can be reinvested in the business, but rational owners only do that when they expect that the investment will cause the business to release even more cash in the future (which can then be used for other things).

Now, profit is not a quantity; it's a rate. A rate is a relationship between two quantities. Profit is the *cash* that is released by a business in a given *time* period. Profit is denominated in units of time. If the period isn't specified, it's implied.

It's helpful to compare the concept of *profit* with *velocity*.

***

Velocity is also a rate: the relationship between distance and time. However, there's a difference. We never use *velocity* as a synonym for *distance*. However, the word *profit* is frequently used to refer to a quantity (cash) as well as a rate (cash/time). This is unfortunate. The former usage leads to confusion and, frequently, poor decisions.

***

The next obvious question is, how do you calculate profit? Profit is NOT revenue minus cost. Profit is the difference between two rates:
1. The rate at which a business generates contribution margin
2. The rate at which that business accrues operating cost

The difference between these two is profit: the *rate* at which a business generates cash.

I'll say it one more time for good measure: profit is not a quantity. It's a rate. *(Cash over time.)*

The time dimension is critically important to business. The moment we forget about time is the moment our business begins to decay.

THE FORGETTING OF TIME, INSTITUTIONALIZED

To use a fancy turn of phrase, cost accounting abstracts away the concept of time.

When a decision is made to allocate some portion of an operating cost to a transaction, a relationship between that cost and transaction volume is assumed and then forgotten!

From that point forward, whenever a manager makes a decision using a *fully loaded* cost, they inherit someone else's assumption without question. And they are, in all likelihood, making a decision that will cause a change in transaction volume that renders the initial assumption invalid!

Now, you might wonder how a business benefits from removing time from consideration and focusing only on cost.

There are two benefits. The first is *ease of use*. The second is *cost containment*, a byproduct of *ease of use*.

Ease of use

It should be obvious that nothing good will come from ignoring operating costs when making day-to-day management decisions. So, cost allocation does at least ensure that operating costs are considered when managers make decisions at the transaction level.

And ease of use is a big deal.

Managers need some method to estimate the organization-wide profit implications of the decisions they are asked to make on a day-to-day basis.

It isn't practical for them to use calculus to reconcile the two different rates that determine profitability. Nor is it practical for them to consult complex mathematical models of the entire organization.

It's unfortunate that cost accounting has a tendency to generate wrong (often wildly wrong) answers, but ease of use is definitely a benefit!

If we are to provide managers with an alternative approach to management decision-making, *ease of use* is a critical attribute.

Chapter 4
THE DIRECTION OF THE SOLUTION

The following (fictitious) story illustrates the conflict between a manager whose intuition is furnishing her with a correct answer in conflict with a directive from the organization's cost accountant.

It also points us toward an alternative approach to management decision-making.

***

A young manager operating an airline ticket counter is approached by an anxious traveler just as she is about to close the flight. The traveler offers to buy a ticket on that flight for $100 (one-third of the standard fare), if any seats are available.

The manager's intuition tells her to take the money and let the traveler grab the one remaining seat on that flight. She knows that this is the last opportunity to sell that seat. She also knows that all meals have been loaded already, meaning there are no incremental costs associated with the sale of that seat.

But she denies the traveler the seat. She recalls a visit from a regional manager who talked about the airline's operating costs. The regional manager explained that the airline's operating expenses were equivalent to $250 per seat on every flight. This meant that around half the passengers on a typical flight were loss-making passengers. Our young manager tells herself that she just saved the airline $150, even though this conclusion seems intuitively wrong.

***

There is no shortage of stories like this that highlight the laughably incorrect answers that can be furnished by cost-based reasoning.

But, rather than laughing at cost accountants, a better use of this story (and others like it) is to ask *why* the correct answer is so obvious. What is it, specifically, about this story that causes the manager's intuition to be *obviously* more accurate than the cost accountant's math?

And, if we can extract a lesson from this story, can we generalize it and package it so as to provide managers with a viable alternative to cost-based reasoning?

A Rosetta stone

In the story above, it's easy to see that the last remaining seat on the outbound plane was a unit of capacity that was about to expire. The traveler's offer would have generated contribution margin for the airline with no corresponding increase in operating cost.

The key insight is that the traveler's proposal would have increased the yield on a capacity-constrained resource. Accordingly, all additional contribution margin would have dropped straight to the bottom line.

Here's a general conclusion that we can draw from the story.

If we can identify the resource that limits the rate at which contribution margin is generated, then we can use the productivity of this resource as a proxy for the profitability of the organization.

It's time now to introduce a couple of terms that will simplify this discussion.

***

Let's use the word Throughput (capital "T") in place of contribution margin. Throughput is revenue minus totally variable costs. (Totally variable costs exclude direct labor, which does not vary in direct proportion to transaction volume.) Additionally, Throughput can be used more generally to refer to a unit of value.

Let's use the word Constraint (capital "C") to refer to the resource that limits the rate at which Throughput is generated.

***

We can now introduce a formula that's an alternative to the standard cost-accounting formula.

$$\Delta \frac{T}{Cu} = \Delta \, Profit$$

(T is Throughput. Cu is a Constraint unit.)

This formula tells us that a change in *Throughput per Constraint Unit* is equal to the change in the organization's profitability.

A manager can use this formula to make a management decision so long as they are confident that the proposal will not cause the Constraint to move to another resource.

***

If we return to our airline counter manager and assume the plane has 175 seats, the traveler's proposal (if accepted) would cause T/Cu to increase by $0.57. (This assumes that 174 seats each generate Throughput of $300, and one generates $100.) Consequently, the airline's profitability would increase by $100 over the period under consideration.

***

The *delta T/Cu* formula is a *Rosetta Stone* that enables a manager to predict, with impressive accuracy, the impact that day-to-day decisions will have on profitability.

Is this insight useful?

I can anticipate your objection, but before I address it, let me point you to an organization that uses this method to make critical management decisions.

That organization is an airline!

If you have had any exposure to airlines (including as a customer), you already know that airlines *do not* use cost accounting to make decisions of the type described in the story above.

Airlines adopted dynamic pricing in the early 1980s and have been fine-tuning it ever since.

Dynamic pricing is based on exactly the logic described above. It recognizes that seats on aircraft (in conjunction with cargo hold space) are the resource that limits the rate at which the airline generates contribution margin. Pricing decisions are made explicitly so as to maximize that yield.

Increasingly, hotels are doing the same thing.

Now, your objection, I suspect, might be that the proposed approach to management decision-making will not work for many organizations because it's impossible to identify the specific resource, at any point in time, that is limiting Throughput.

Now, this is true. But it doesn't have to be.

The reason the Constraint location is unpredictable in most organizations is that organizations are managed with a view to minimizing cost rather than maximizing speed.

The relentless minimization of cost within an organization is beneficial up to a point, after which it causes the organization to become chaotic, meaning that it causes the Constraint to move unpredictably from resource to resource.

Once the organization becomes chaotic, whatever increases in profitability are generated by cost reduction are eliminated by a sudden decrease in the rate at which the organization generates Throughput.

And this is terrible news!

When the rate at which an organization generates Throughput slows, the rate at which the organization delivers value to its customers also slows.

Practically, this means that every customer interaction runs slower. It takes longer to get a quote. It takes longer to get an order filled. And it takes longer to get an issue resolved. This means that the organization has become less competitive.

If an organization is managed with a view to maximizing speed, it will never be allowed to become chaotic—meaning that the Constraint will *not* move unpredictably from resource to resource.

SPEED AS AN ANTIDOTE TO CHAOS

There's a very simple (and incredibly important) reason for this.

When it comes to generating Throughput, not all resources are equal. For each unit of available capacity, a few make a vastly greater contribution than others.

***

For example, if you own a printing business, you will be more profitable when your million-dollar printing press is fully activated and your design team is out to lunch than you will be when your design team is heavily loaded, and the press is sitting idle.

***

If your goal is to maximize the rate at which your organization generates profit, it's incumbent upon you to first identify your *printing press:* that resource that makes the most significant contribution to your organization's profitability (per unit of capacity). You should then design your organization to ensure that this resource is:

1. Consistently fully activated
2. Loaded with the mix work that generates the highest *Throughput per Constraint unit*

Once you have anchored your Constraint at its optimal location, the airline metaphor above suddenly becomes relevant. You can then use *delta T/Cu* to predict the profit implications of most day-to-day management decisions.

The Direction Of The Solution

Our Documentary: Double-Digit Growth

If you're aiming for double-digit growth but consistently end up settling for singles, this documentary explains why (and, what to do about it).

SCAN TO WATCH

bit.ly/3YAjb8c

Chapter 5
THE SOLUTION: THROUGHPUT-BASED REASONING

Every meaningful management decision involves a prediction.

In a large, complex organization, *effects* are separated by both space and time from their *causes*.

When a manager considers a simple proposal (for example, *should I offer a discount for a bulk purchase*), their job is to try and predict the consequences of that proposal. And, ultimately, the consequence that really matters is the impact on the profitability of the organization.

So, cost-based reasoning is a means of making predictions. Throughput-based reasoning, proposed here, is an alternative.

The obvious questions, then, are which is the easiest to use and which has the greatest predictive power?

Two approaches to predictions

Cost-based reasoning excels when it comes to ease of use. You simply subtract the change in revenue from the change in fully loaded costs to arrive at the predicted change in profit.

Throughput-based reasoning requires that you calculate *Throughput per Constraint unit* for both the current and the proposed scenarios. The difference between the two is the predicted change in profit.

To determine if these additional steps are worthwhile, let's consider the predictive power of both approaches.

Cost-based reasoning proceeds from the assumption that operating costs vary in direct proportion to transaction volume. If you sell one more unit, your operating costs increment accordingly.

We know this is wrong. The relationship between operating costs and volume is a step function. As you sell more units, operating costs remain unchanged until suddenly, they don't!

This is consequential for two very important reasons. First, we cannot assume that the scale of an organization smoothes out this step function. Costs ratchet up periodically, but under normal circumstances, they don't ratchet back down.

And, second, in a competitive market, profit is generated *at the margins.* What this means is that most of the Throughput generated by a large number of transactions pays down operating costs. The difference between being *just profitable* and *very profitable* comes down to just a few *additional* transactions. Cost-based reasoning actually obscures the outsized profit contribution made by those additional transactions.

The power of Throughput-based reasoning is that it recognizes the true nature of the relationship between Throughput and operating costs. It recognizes that these are not two independent variables (like a person running up a down elevator). It recognizes that, within a non-chaotic organization, there is a predictable relationship between a change in volume and a change in profitability.

The key to understanding this relationship is to recognize the reason why operating costs exist. Operating costs are the cost of our organization's capacity: the capacity to do work and, consequently, to generate Throughput (either directly or indirectly).

Because we know that the profitability of an organization increases when Throughput increases relative to operating costs, then we can conclude that profitability is proportional to the yield on capacity.

In most organizations, this observation is correct but useless! Operating costs pay for all kinds of capacity (machines, real estate, insurance policies, HR departments, and so on). It's simply impossible to reconcile the capacity of the organization with a unit of Throughput.

However, as discussed earlier, when an organization is managed for speed, management will act to ensure that the resource that makes the largest incremental profit contribution is fully loaded at all times.

When the organization is operating in this state it becomes easy to understand the relationship between Throughput and capacity. We can disregard all resources other than the Constraint, divide the capacity of the Constraint into units of useful work, and then simply estimate how many Constraint units will be consumed in order to fulfil each order.

Now that we understand the relationship between Throughput and capacity (and, accordingly, between Throughput and operating costs), we can quickly and accurately predict the (organization-wide) profit implication of most proposals.

A SIMPLE, BOTTOM-UP APPROACH TO MANAGEMENT DECISIONS

Throughput-based reasoning (unlike the alternative) empowers operators to make bold decisions: those critical decisions that have an outsized impact on the organization's profitability.

If the location of the Constraint is obvious to operators, Throughput-based reasoning is intuitive. However, if the organization has been allowed to descend into a chaotic state, operators have no choice but to retreat to the relative safety of cost-based decision-making.

Accordingly, it is the responsibility of senior management to design the organization in such a way that the Constraint remains anchored at its optimal location by sufficient *protective capacity* at all other resources.

Senior management can also assist operators by identifying and visualizing metrics that reflect the contribution (positive or negative) that operators' work is making to the productivity of the Constraint.

Upstream from the Constraint, metrics should be designed to ensure that the Constraint is never starved of work, and downstream, metrics should ensure that a unit of value generated at the Constraint is never wasted.

Obviously, operators should not be allowed to make decisions that will cause the Constraint to move. (We've all seen the catastrophic effect on airlines when a technology problem causes the Constraint to shift from their fleet of aircraft to the reservation system!)

However, in a healthy, well-designed organization, it should be very difficult to move the Constraint.

Containing costs

It should not be assumed that a shift in management focus from cost to speed is a license to spend indiscriminately. The overriding goal, obviously, is the generation of profit.

Raw-material costs are always considered in the calculation of contribution margin and any proposal to increase operating cost should be treated similar to an investment proposal.

The containment of costs is like wearing hearing protection on the plant floor. It's not the goal, but it's certainly a necessary condition.

The major difference in this new environment is a heightened awareness of the importance of protective capacity. An idle machine (or person) is adding value if they are preventing the Constraint from becoming idle. Think about it: you wouldn't downsize your district's fire brigade if you discovered that firefighters weren't actually extinguishing fires 24 hours a day!

Chapter 6
TWO CRITICAL VALUE CHAINS

There's another insidious way that cost accounting damages businesses. By abstracting away the concept of time, the cost-based approach to decision-making obscures the fact that businesses contain processes (or value chains) that must be decoupled.

By *decoupled*, I mean that they must operate with a high degree of independence.

Healthy businesses contain two such value chains. (I'm favoring the term *value chain* rather than *process* because these processes span multiple departments):

1. The first value chain generates *Throughput*.
2. The second value chain generates *growth* (a positive change in Throughput).

The *Throughput* value chain consists of the sequence of activities required to convert a customer's order into money in the bank. (The various departments that perform these activities are typically members of the operations group.)

The *growth* value chain consists of the activities required to increase the rate at which customer orders are received. (The departments that contribute to growth include *sales, new product development, quality,* and *acquisitions*.)

If you consider the departments that contribute to growth, two things are clear. First, in most organizations, these departments are not managed as part of a distinct group. And, second, in most organizations, individuals within these departments are responsible for activities across both value chains.

For example, salespeople are frequently responsible for solving customer problems, and engineers are often responsible for both new product development and the processing of customers' special orders.

The problem with sharing resources between these two value chains is that whenever there is resource contention between the two, the *Throughput* chain will win. Under these conditions, unless you have a lot of protective capacity (which is unlikely when cost-based decision-making is prevalent), what tends to happen is that the level of effort allocated to growth quickly goes to zero!

A better approach is to manage these two value chains as distinct groups. Each has its own goal. Each will have its own Constraint. And each will have its own set of metrics. If resources absolutely have to be shared between these two groups, those resources should have a lot of protective capacity and they should be formally scheduled to avoid contention.

Of course, these two groups are not fully independent—they are nested, like Russian dolls—but they should be managed independently. Money spent on growth should be treated like an investment, not a normal cost. This is because the output of this group (the addition of a new customer, the acquisition of a competitor's business, or the commercialization of a new product line) is a new stream of Throughput that will persist for many normal reporting cycles.

Two Critical Value Chains

Chapter 7
AN INTRODUCTION TO METRICS

Eli Goldratt would often say, "Tell me how you'll measure me, and I'll tell you how I'll behave."

This idea should not be controversial, given that a metric is just a form of feedback. All but the most simple tasks require that the operator make regular adjustments to their work based on the evidence of their senses.

The purpose of a metric is to either augment or replace the operator's senses (pilots, for example, learn to trust their instruments over their senses).

Metrics should be designed to synchronize the behavior of operators with the goal of the organization. A Kanban bin system is a perfect example of this in a production environment. If parts are present in a bin, the operator will process those parts, and when the bin is empty, they stop. The bin prevents overproduction and, more likely than not, results in the operator working faster when there's actually work to be done.

Importantly, the Kanban system improves the profitability of the organization by causing the operator to be *less efficient!*

A SYSTEM OF METRICS

It's beneficial for the executive team to carefully design a system of metrics for the organization rather than inheriting traditional metrics or trusting that line management will select metrics that result in operators subordinating effectively to the goal of the organization.

Ideally, each department should have a single metric for value creation (or *key performance indicator*) and one or two *necessary conditions* that must be respected. The most effective key performance indicators (KPIs) are compound measurements that, under normal circumstances, make additional measurements redundant. (For example, if a production department is consistently averaging 95% on-time-delivery performance, we can assume that the assembly line is not suffering from unscheduled downtime.)

Your system of metrics should have a hierarchical structure.

At the top of the hierarchy, there's a single metric that subsumes both the profitability and the growth of the business. That metric is *enterprise value* (or stock price, averaged over a sensible timeframe).

At the next level, we have the two value chains that drive profitability and growth. The metrics for these will be *Throughput per period* and *new-business value per period*, respectively. In both cases, the *period* should be the shortest sensible timeframe. Ideally a *day* (not a quarter!). *New-business value* is the net present value of new business won (think of the *lifetime value* of a new account, for example).

Now, each of these value chains will contain a nominated Constraint. Accordingly, metrics for each department within these value chains should be set with respect to the Constraint. Generally speaking, activities upstream should replenish the Constraint as rapidly as possible (so it is never starved of work), and activities downstream should ensure that work done at the constraint is converted to value rapidly (so the Constraint's capacity is not wasted).

So, as an example, if we consider the procurement department in an engineer-to-order production environment, we might conclude that the role of procurement is to ensure that all inputs for jobs are received prior to the scheduled release. However, we would also recognize that building parts inventories is undesirable. Consequently, we might measure the percentage of procured parts that arrive during a pre-release *Goldilocks zone.*

Such a metric would penalize both late deliveries and inventory building and would encourage the development of healthy supplier relationships and the micro-management of those suppliers with less-than-optimal historical performance.

If you've ever spent time in a procurement department in a cost-focused organization, you'll appreciate that these are not common behaviors!

The shockingly effective approach to selling into project environments

This video explains why you should pursue projects and not people in order to drive rapid growth.

SCAN TO WATCH

bit.ly/3UnIU0S

Chapter 8
RETOOLING FOR SPEED

The move from cost- to Throughput-based reasoning does not start by teaching operators new operating procedures. It starts with:
1. A commitment to speed, rather than cost, as the basis for optimization
2. A redesign of the organization to anchor the Constraint locations

The former requires that you read (and maybe reread) this paper and, ideally, the additional resources referenced.

The latter is a more significant undertaking. First, you need to determine the resource (or set of resources) that should be the Constraint (for your *Throughput* value chain). If you're not sure, your Constraint should probably be the resource that makes the biggest contribution to your competitive advantage (as well as to profitability) when it is fully activated.

You will then need to change the way that work is planned within your organization so as to force your nominated resource to become the Constraint. The transition from chaos to a single Constraint must happen quickly (definitely within 30 days).

And then, when the transition is made, you can turn your attention to your system of metrics and your plan to drive growth and, accordingly, the design of your *growth* value chain.

In a typical organization, these first two steps involve a *significant* amount of work. But, if you have a commitment to growth, you must compare the level of effort associated with this approach with the level of effort demanded by the cost-focused alternative.

Chapter 9
AN ODE TO SPEED: PART 2

At the start of this paper, I stated that if I were to give a single piece of advice to the owner of an industrial business, it would be to *increase your organization's clock speed.*

I truly mean that. A business that runs faster is a business that delivers more value to its customers and generates more profit for its owners. Furthermore, a business that runs faster also grows faster.

The widespread adoption of cost accounting has removed the time dimension from day-to-day decision-making and has contorted the mental model that informs most managers' intuition.

If you want to outgrow your competitors, it's critical that you reintroduce the time dimension to decision-making throughout your organization.

Chapter 10

CODA: TWO EXAMPLES OF THROUGHPUT-BASED DECISION-MAKING

How should a manufacturer of countertops price a new product

A manufacturer fabricates countertops from engineered stone for commercial projects. They have developed a range of sinks that can be fabricated from the same material as the countertop. They need to know how to price these sinks.

There are four critical pieces of information this manufacturer should collect to make this decision:

1. What is the price that the market is paying for comparable sinks?
2. What are the totally-variable costs associated with the sink?
3. What is the current yield (T/Cu) at the Constraint?
4. How many units of Constraint capacity will be consumed in order to fill an order for a sink?

Let's assume that the market is paying $1,000 for comparable sinks. Let's also assume that the raw-material cost will be just $100 (we predict that 60% of the stone will be scrap from countertop production that would otherwise be discarded).

Let's assume that this manufacturer's Constraint is its installation crew. This would imply that the manufacturer programs the plant operation around the availability of the crew. With careful programming, we'll assume that the crew can do two installations a day.

The current yield on the Constraint (T/CU) is the total Throughput for a standard period, divided by the number of installations over that period. If we assume the crew averages 9 installations a week (one half-day is lost to callbacks), and that the total Throughput generated over that period is $47,250, then an average Constraint unit is yielding $5,250.

If we assume that it takes the installation crew 60 minutes to install a sink, then this is a lot less than the half-day Constraint Unit. But, there's a danger that, in some cases, the additional time required for sink installation will prevent the crew from doing a second installation that day. In these cases, the sink installation consumes an entire Constraint unit. If this occurs just twice a week, then the sale of each sink generates $900 in Throughput but decreases T/Cu by $467.

Under these circumstances, the manufacturer would need to charge at least $1,467 for the sink just to maintain current profitability, which makes these sinks a questionable proposition.

However, the manufacturer should consider some additional options:

1. They could take steps to reduce the sink installation time and eliminate the risk of the installation consuming an additional Constraint unit.
2. They could sell sinks direct-to-consumer, which would would place no load on their Constraint.

3. Additionally, the manufacturer might consider having a separate specialist perform callbacks. After all, it's unlikely that callbacks require exactly the same set of skills as installations.

The profit implications of the four scenarios presented here are wildly divergent. However, the important point is that this analysis would not normally be performed in an environment where cost-based decision-making is prevalent.

The danger of the departmental profit and loss statement

A year ago, a large commercial plumbing firm acquired a small manufacturer of pre-fabricated plumbing racks.

These prefabricated racks dramatically reduce the time it takes for a plumber to install bathrooms and kitchens in large projects (like hotels).

The plumbing firm's assumption was that the manufacturing business would increase the productivity of its commercial plumbers (a limited and expensive resource) and generate some additional profits by selling its products to other plumbing firms.

A recent review of the performance of the acquisition revealed that the expected productivity improvements had not been realized. The only good (but somewhat concerning) news was that the manufacturing division was selling more units to competitive plumbing firms than expected.

The problem was that the manufacturing division continued operating autonomously after the acquisition. Specifically, it generated its own profit and loss statement and sold its products to the larger plumbing firm at market value.

Because the manufacturing division was attempting to maximize its profitability, it kept costs low (which limited capacity) and sold its products to the highest bidder. Because supply was limited, project managers within the larger plumbing firm had concluded that the division was an unreliable supplier and were electing to have plumbers do their own fabrication on-site.

The root cause of this problem is a failure to properly integrate the manufacturer into the larger organization. It should not have been allowed to operate autonomously, and it should definitely not have been expected to generate its own profit and loss statement.

The larger plumbing firm should have held its new manufacturing division accountable to a metric that drove proper subordination. The identification of this metric requires an understanding of the Constraint within the larger enterprise.

If (as is likely the case) the Constraint is the plumbing firm's pool of qualified plumbers, proper subordination would mean ensuring that prefabricated racks could be delivered to building sites whenever required (without the requirement for quotations or purchase orders!).

The metric for the manufacturing division would be on-time delivery performance, which means that the manufacturer would be forced to maintain protective capacity to accommodate variability in demand.

This protective capacity would inflate the manufacturing division's costs relative to the autonomous mode of operation, but some of these costs could be offset by using downtime to manufacture units for sale in the open marketplace.

These changes would result in the enterprise Constraint becoming more productive, causing a direct increase in Throughput. The acquisition would perform as expected if the increase in Throughput is meaningfully larger than the manufacturing-related operating expenses.

Interestingly, it would make total sense for the plumbing firm's finance department to use cost-accounting methods to analyze the commercial viability of the acquisition both before and after the fact.

But it makes no sense whatsoever to use cost-based logic to make day-to-day management decisions. In addition to generating incorrect results, the resulting cost-based mental model will create a gravitational pull toward the atomization of the organization (the presumption of profits at the level of divisions, product lines, and transactions).

Further reading

If this paper resonates, you really must read *The Goal* (Eliyahu Goldratt). This is one of the best-selling business books ever written, and it does a spectacular job of explaining the concept of the *Constraint*.

If you're looking for an exhaustive exploration of cost-based reasoning, your next stop is *Throughput Economics* (Eli Schragenheim, Henry Fitzhugh Camp, and Rocco Surace).

And, if you'd like a break from reading, you might like to watch our video documentary *(Double-Digit Growth)* here: www.ballistix.com/resources.

Assistance is available

Justin and the Ballistix team create and actively participate in Steering Committees for a small number of organizations. These Steering Committees are dedicated to transitioning those organizations to what we call a Speed-Based Operating System.

If you'd like an overview of this service offering, please send a request to mattie.hayden@ballistix.com

Watch the Sales Documentary on YouTube

**Our Documentary:
Double-Digit Growth**

If you're aiming for double-digit growth but consistently end up settling for singles, this documentary explains why (and, what to do about it).

SCAN TO WATCH

bit.ly/3YAjb8c

BONUS CONTENT

DOUBLE-DIGIT GROWTH

(AND WHY YOU'RE STUCK ON SINGLE DIGITS)

JUSTIN ROFF-MARSH

INTRODUCTION

Most industrial businesses aim for double-digit annual growth. Why, then, do they end up settling for single digits?

The owners of most industrial businesses aim for double-digit growth.

But each year, because of a simple design flaw, they end up settling for single digits.

I'm going to take you on a journey, back to the 1950s, to highlight the design flaw that's (most likely) limiting *your* business to single-digit growth. On our journey we'll stop in on Ray Kroc, prior to his adventure with Mcdonalds and then we'll visit the Xerox Corporation, where we'll find the solution to your growth problem, hiding in plain sight!

But, before we climb into our little time machine, let's agree on why it make sense to pursue double-digit growth.

In my experience the difference between single-digit growth and double digits is the difference between a workforce on cruise control, versus an energized organization.

It's the difference between steady profits for the owners, versus surplus cashflow that can be used to fund innovation and the pursuit of even more aggressive growth.

And it's the difference, ultimately, between being acquired, versus being the acquirer.

There's a reason I want to take you back to the 1950s. This was the decade where a fundamental change in the relationship between companies and their customers came into sharp focus. This change resulted in the traditional design of an organization's front-of-house being replaced with an entirely different model. But, as I've hinted already, this change—fundamental though it was—has basically been ignored for the last 60 years.

1954

1954 was the year that Ray Kroc sold a milkshake machine to the first Mcdonald's restaurant in California. If you've seen the 2016 movie, *The Founder*, you'll remember Ray Kroc lugging machines from restaurant to restaurant, demoing these machines, in the hopes of securing orders.

This is a pretty accurate representation of the 1950s sales department. Back then there was a simple division of responsibilities between Production and Sales. In the case of Prince Castle, where Ray Kroc worked, the Production department manufactured Multimixers and the Sales department was responsible for selling them.

Production folks were responsible for product. And salespeople were responsible for revenue.

Now, by making Ray Kroc responsible for revenue, Prince Castle ensured that Ray Kroc became their customers' primary interface with the organization. Which is to say, Ray Kroc WAS Prince Castle's front-of-house.

It may not seem significant now, but I'd like you to remember that point. By making a salesperson responsible for revenue, Prince Castle guaranteed that that salesperson would become their organization's front-of-house.

Of course Ray Kroc and his relationship with the McDonald brothers would turn out to be transformative. But that's a different story.

The transformation I want to highlight here occurred at the end of that decade.

1959

In 1959, on the other coast of America, Xerox introduced its pay-per-copy proposition, along with the revolutionary 914 copier. This copier was 100 times faster than the average copier at the time, but it was expensive. Really expensive!

The pay-per-copy proposition allowed Xerox to sell copying as a service (just 4c a copy!). This made copiers affordable and it catapulted Xerox into a position of absolute market dominance—a position it held until it was forced to license its patent portfolio in the 70s.

Now consider pay-per-copy from a Xerox salesperson's perspective. With this proposition, the salesperson was no longer directly responsible for revenue, as they were with the traditional capital-equipment sale.

The salesperson was essentially responsible for selling a service. And, revenue was a product of that service, not directly a product of the salesperson's endeavors.

With pay-per-copy there were now two classes of transaction. There was the sale of the service and then there was the sale that occurred every time someone pressed the copy button. The first class of transaction generated a signed contract (but no revenue). It was the second class of transaction that generated revenue.

Suddenly, it was no longer correct to say that the Xerox salesperson generated revenue. The salesperson sold the copier and the copier generated revenue.

Now, it would be tempting to say that this is a *distinction without a difference.* But, to draw this conclusion would be to ignore the ugly truth about the Xerox 914 copier.

As anyone who had the pleasure of working in an office in the 20th Century will attest, photocopiers were frequently broken. It was common for a queue of office workers to form, waiting for the Xerox technician to finish dragging crumpled sheets of copypaper from the labyrinth of rollers inside the machine.

If there was a person at Xerox who directly influenced revenue it was most certainly not the salesperson: it was the field technician!

It turns out that Xerox didn't just invent the modern copier, Xerox also pioneered the modern approach to field technical support!

From the Xerox customer's perspective, the field technician was now their primary interface with the organization, not the salesperson. In fact, I'm pretty sure, if you asked any Xerox customer, last century, who from Xerox they would most like to visit them, they would answer, without hesitation, a technician!

THE LESSON

So, in our journey back to the 1950s, I introduced you to two technologies and the responsibilities of the salespeople who sold them.

In the case of the milkshake machine, Ray Kroc sold them for the Prince Castle corporation and he was directly responsible for the generation of revenue.

But in the case of the Xerox 914 copier, salespeople sold a service that incorporated the copier—but they were *not* directly responsible for the generation of revenue.

I have a question for you. Which of these cases is more relevant to the modern industrial sales environment?

What do you think? My answer is both (or, perhaps, neither).

In the modern industrial sales environment, we sell propositions that are more similar to the Xerox one. However we maintain sales departments that look just like the one that employed Ray Kroc, back when he was selling milkshake machines.

And THIS is why your industrial organization is stuck on single-digit growth!

I'm going to explain, at length, how to fix this problem. But first, let me fortify the claim I just made. After all, unless you feel like my position is warranted there's no value in my proposed solution.

The first part of my claim is that industrial organizations, today, sell propositions that are more similar to the Xerox one.

My assertion is that, over time, new technologies transition from being sold as discrete products to being sold as services. This is obviously the case with the photocopier, also things like electricity generation and computing infrastructure. But it's less obvious if we consider more mundane technologies like nuts and bolts, or even toilet paper.

But, if you think about it, in a business context, we don't make discrete purchases of commodity products like nuts and bolts or toilet paper. We might pay for them discretely but we enter into a commercial relationship with a supplier we trust to provide these and perhaps hundreds of similar products. In the case of nuts and bolts, that supplier might be Grainger or Fastenal. In the case of toilet paper, it might be Staples. We might audit those suppliers periodically to ensure their prices are fair but, for the most part, discrete commodity purchases are programmatic.

This means that today, salespeople do not, for the most part, directly influence revenue. The role of salespeople *should be* to sell the overarching commercial relationships, from which revenue will flow.

However—and this brings me to the second part of my claim—most sales departments are structured today as if salespeople are directly responsible for generating revenue.

In fact, if you ask business owners and executives which of their departments is responsible for revenue the answer is ALWAYS the same: the Sales department.

And if you look at how salespeople are compensated, in almost every case, salespeople's incomes are tied to the revenue that emerges, on a month-to-month basis, from those accounts that they have won historically.

WHAT COULD POSSIBLY GO WRONG?

Now this sounds harmless enough, right?

But let me expose the folly of this hybrid approach with one simple question. Are you ready?

What do you think would have happened in the late 1950s if Xerox had made their salespeople directly responsible for photocopier revenue?

That's right, in short order, all of their salespeople would have devolved into highly-paid service technicians—and, before long, no one would have been selling copiers.

Even with Xerox's best-in-class fleet of field technicians, if Xerox was silly enough to make salespeople directly responsible for revenue, those salespeople would have proceeded, en mass, to the nearest hardware store to kit themselves out with wrenches, rubber gloves, and multimeters.

Do you see where I'm going with this?

In the modern industrial organization, salespeople are still directly responsible for revenue and, consequently, they have devolved, over time, into highly-paid, field-based, providers of technical services.

The modern industrial salesperson is a salesperson in name only. They are part customer service rep, part technical specialist, part project manager, and part trainer. The only connection most have to sales is the sense of guilt they experience as they drive home each day! By making your salespeople responsible for revenue you have made salespeople your primary customer interface—your front-of-house. And by making salespeople your front-of-house you have consigned your organization to single-digit growth.

REVENUE: FOUR BASIC TRUTHS

Before we talk about the solution to this problem, we need to have a frank and honest discussion about revenue. I've hinted at what I'm about to tell you but this is so important that it really needs to be stated explicitly.

TRUTH #1: SALESPEOPLE DO NOT GENERATE REVENUE

Salespeople—when they're effective—generate commercial relationships. And commercial relationships generate revenue.

Now, commercial relationships, when they're established, are often accompanied by an order. That order is only significant because it's evidence of the new commercial relationship. The revenue associated with that order is incidental.

TRUTH #2: OPERATIONS—NOT SALES–*DOES* GENERATE REVENUE

Make no mistake, revenue IS important. You need it. You need it to make payroll. You need it to invest in new-product development and innovation. And you and your fellow shareholders need it to fund your rock-n-roll lifestyles!

So revenue is critically important. But it doesn't come from the sales department, it comes from Operations. If you're not sure I'm correct, do this simple test. Make a list of the last 10 customers who defected and took their business to a competitor. Review each case and determine why each left.

My guess is they *all* defected for one of three reasons. Either, they were unhappy with your delivery performance. Or, they were unhappy with your pricing. Or, they were unhappy with your product (or range of products, perhaps).

These are the standard three reasons why industrial organizations lose customers: delivery performance, pricing and product. And ALL are the direct responsibility of Operations. Salespeople do not directly control any of these.

Truth #3: In economic terms, customer relationships (or accounts) are annuities

This is an important concept. An annuity is a series of future payments. From your bank's perspective, the mortgage they sold you is an annuity.

If you have a rental property, the agreement you have with your tenant is an annuity. When Xerox sold the 914 copier, those 4c transactions were an annuity.

Because it's inconvenient for your customers to change suppliers frequently (you know, switching cost), each of your customer relationships is an annuity—regardless of whether or not the relationship is codified with a contract. In fact, if you have a decent-sized basket of accounts, the law of large numbers enables you to make pretty accurate predictions about the purchasing behavior of a typical account.

Truth #4: The value of an account is inversely proportional to its cumulative spend

So, if in economic terms, an account is an annuity, it turns out there's a formula you can use to calculate its value. It's called the Net Present Value calculation. Basically, net present value is the sum of future payments, discounted back to today's dollars.

Unfortunately, few executives have bothered to calculate the net-present-value of a typical account. I say "unfortunately" because, if you do the math, you're likely to get a pleasant surprise.

A new account that spends just a few thousand dollars a month will most likely have a net-present-value in the tens of thousands of dollars—and that's assuming you do your calculations based on contribution margin, not revenue.

However, as time passes, and potential revenue is converted into actual revenue, the economic value of the account actually reduces.

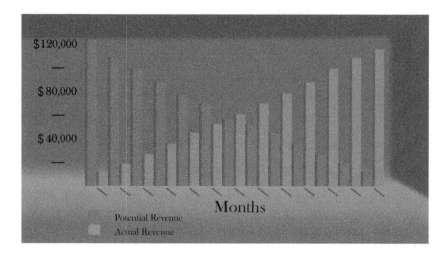

This means that an account is worth the most, the day it's won—even though the account has not yet generated a single dollar in revenue.

If there was a number that you should be celebrating in your Sales Department, it's the net-present-value of new business won—not the monthly revenue receipts.

ADRIFT FROM REALITY

Of course, this is the EXACT OPPOSITE of how every industrial organization conceptualizes the contribution their sales department makes to the enterprise. And this fundamental misunderstanding of Sales results in a litany of bad decisions.

In fact, it won't hurt to count them!

1. We hold salespeople accountable for revenue, even though they don't directly influence it, and even though this distracts them from the pursuit of new business.
2. We pay them commissions, based on revenue, which focuses them, even more sharply, on exactly the set of behaviors we DON'T want them to engage in.
3. We underresourced Operations, based on the assumption that salespeople should responsible for revenue.
4. We miscalculate the value of new business and, consequently, underinvest in the growth of our enterprises.

These are significant problems that emerge from a casual disregard for the fundamental nature of an industrial organization.

This disregard almost rises to the level of fraud. But you don't have to worry. You're not going to do hard time—this is a fraud you're committing against yourself!

THE DESIGN FLAW AND HOW TO FIX IT

Fortunately, this problem is pretty easy to fix—in theory. (It's a little more complicated in practice.)

In theory, we begin by updating our starting assumption.

We recognize that salespeople do not directly generate—and should not be held accountable for—revenue.

This means that Operations must accept responsibility for revenue—and this forces us to rethink the design of our organization.

In Ray Kroc's time, the Prince Castle organization looked kind of like this.

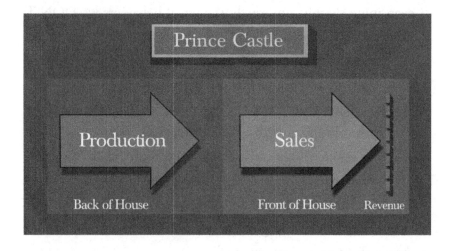

In the back-of-house you had production, making stuff. Then, in the front-of-house, facing the customer, you had the sales department, generating revenue.

There are two important points here.

First, we're looking at a single process. Price Castle manufactures a machine. Ray Kroc sells it. Second, Sales and the front-of-house are synonymous. The Prince Castle salesperson IS the organization's customer interface.

But now, if we visualize the Xerox model, both of those things change.

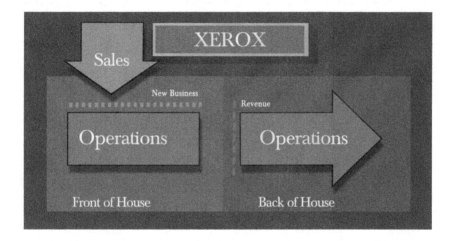

Where, previously, we had one process, we now have two. And the salesperson is no longer the customer's primary interface with the organization.

You can see that I've replaced Production with Operations. Operations is the value chain that stretches from the receipt of an order to fulfillment. So, it includes production, along with customer service, purchasing, logistics, and so on.

In the Xerox model, Operations is fully responsible for the generation of revenue. Within Operations, you have some departments that are customer-facing (customer service and technical support, for example), and, of course, we still have purchasing, production, and logistics in the back-of-house.

So the first process is the process that generates revenue and Operations is responsible for that entire process. The second process is the process that generates new business. And that is the sole responsibility of Sales.

Now, these are two discrete processes, which is to say that Sales has minimal dependence on Operations, and visa versa. This loose coupling between Sales and Operations is the critical attribute of the Xerox model.

And if you want to shift your organization from single- to double-digit growth, you must redesign your front-of-house in line with the Xerox model, which means you MUST ensure that your Sales function is loosely coupled with Operations.

THE MAGIC OF LOOSE COUPLING

A moment ago, I said that the design flaw was easy to fix in theory; more difficult in practice.

The key to fixing this problem in practice is to understand the notion of loose coupling.

For a perfect example of two processes, loosely coupled, within the one system, consider a cyclist on a modern bicycle with a freewheeling gear set.

The cyclist can stand in the saddle and sprint—causing the bicycle to accelerate. But if he tires, returns to his saddle, and stops pedaling, the bicycle continues to travel at its new, higher velocity.

The relationship between the cyclist and the bicycle is exactly the relationship you need to create between your Sales department and Operations.

Sales is the cyclist, who stands and sprints. Operations is the bicycle, that remains in motion, thanks to inertia. And, of course, the motion itself is revenue.

To achieve this special relationship, you must make Operations self-sufficient with respect to revenue generation.

By self-sufficient, I mean that if your customers have an inclination to purchase from you and they know roughly what it is that they want, they should be able to transact with your organization without any involvement from salespeople.

This means that your Operations group should be able to receive inbound inquiries, design solutions, generate proposals, process orders, onboard new customers, and resolve any issues that arise along the way.

If you achieve this level of transactional self-sufficiency in Operations, then—and only then—can you insist that your Sales department focuses exclusively on the pursuit of new business.

By the way, when I say that Sales should focus on new business, I mean new customers and new categories of business for existing customers. Operations should be responsible for incremental growth, or growth within existing categories. This is because customers' spend within categories is primarily a function of Operational performance.

Okay. We'll get to Sales in a minute. First, let me walk you through the four changes you'll need to make to your Operations group to get to transactional self-sufficiency.

CUSTOMER SERVICE

There's a basic trifecta of transactional tasks you need to perform efficiently in order to bank your customers' money and keep it banked.

You need to generate quotes. You need to process orders. And you need to answer questions and resolve issues as they arise.

Your customer service team needs the capability and the capacity to perform 100% of these tasks. And then it needs protective capacity in reserve to ensure that it can still perform them at the end of a busy month—with a couple of operators off sick—at a faster rate and to a higher standard than salespeople can currently perform them.

Realistically, to achieve this, you will need to stop dividing up work for your customer service team by geography, product line, and client, and build one large front-line team of generalist customer service representatives. You will then need to support this generalist team with a second tier of experts who can perform tasks that are too large or too complex to be performed by the tier-one generalists.

With this structure, you should be able to make it significantly easier and faster for customers to transact with you.

ONBOARDING

In industrial organizations, there is often effort associated with the onboarding of new business. This might entail mapping a customer's previous purchases to your stock items and delivering training. Or it might involve integration between enterprise systems—or even the installation of equipment (or people) in your customer's locations.

Whatever the requirements, this work cannot be done by your customer service team. At a minimum, you should have one or more coordinators who specialize in managing customer onboarding—or, if the level of effort justifies it, you should build a self-contained onboarding team.

ENGINEERING

It's amazing (and shocking) that many industrial organizations boast about the quality of technical support they provide to their customers. But then, when you scratch beneath the surface (and trust me, I've done a lot of scratching) you discover that these organizations have no engineering team.

This means one of two things. Either salespeople are currently masquerading as engineers, or these organizations actually have engineers on their sales team, in which case they have engineers masquerading as salespeople.

Neither—believe it or not—is optimal.

A better approach is to put the organization's most technically adept individuals into a central team. If you're struggling to find a name for this department, you might consider … "Engineering", perhaps?!

Your new engineering department can provide technical services to customers (and potential customers) at the behest of both your Customer Service and your Sales teams.

And this department can be managed by a professional Head of Engineering who, presumably will be quite keen to scale both the quantity and quality of services provided.

Now, it may be that you're a manufacturer and you already have an engineering department. If so, you should ensure that this department is split into two teams. Production engineering is production-facing and is concerned with the delivery of orders that have already been won. And Design Engineering is customer-facing, specializing in the design of solutions. You should never have Production and Design engineering tasks performed by a pooled engineering team because these tasks are performed at a materially different cadence and a materially different level of resolution.

ACCOUNT MANAGEMENT

Many industrial salespeople call themselves Account Managers. In most cases, this is a bit of an exaggeration. When you remove the tasks that are now performed by Customer Service, Onboarding, and Engineering, most customers have no additional requirements.

But not all. There are some customers whose vendor relationships are complex enough that they benefit from a kind of concierge service that transcends the day-to-day transactional tasks.

If you have customers who would benefit from such a service, you should certainly provide it. And "Account Manager" is a sensible title for the person who performs this role.

But, be careful here. Because your Account Managers are primarily engaged in the generation of revenue, they are part of your Operations group (not Sales). They will however, generate a steady stream of sales opportunities that can be fed to your Sales team.

AND NOW, TO GROW!

The changes to Operations I've just detailed add up to a significant restructure in most industrial organizations. But these are low-risk, high-value changes that probably should have been made decades ago.

Almost all organizations report an immediate uptick in revenues. A cynical observer might interpret this as evidence that customers never cared that much about long walks on the beach with salespeople—they just wanted their stuff!

But sarcasm aside, the result of these changes is that your organization is now so much easier to deal with, and salespeople now have absolutely nothing to do with their time, other than to pursue new business.

SALES AND MARKETING

You might assume that if you were to remove all distractions from salespeople they would automatically embark on a quest for new business.

The truth is, there are two changes you need to make within the Sales department before salespeople will start to drive the growth you're looking for.

Move your core sales team inside

The first thing you need to do is move your core sales team inside.

It turns out that the lion's share of effort that needs to be expended in order to win new business is expended on the phone or in video conferences—NOT face-to-face with potential customers.

Furthermore, of the conversations that do need to be performed face to face, most of them are technical in nature (most commonly, what's called detailed requirement discovery) meaning that they should be performed by members of your design engineering team, not by salespeople.

Now, it's true that there is a small number of high-value selling conversations that do need to be performed in the field, particularly where large deals are concerned. But you should not have members of your core sales team performing these conversations. It's better to have a small number of highly-capable enterprise salespeople who travel and perform these meetings on behalf of the core sales team. (In a smaller organization, members of the senior executive team can fill this role.)

The reality is that the days of sales as primarily a field-based activity are long gone and they're never coming back. The design of your sales function needs to reflect this reality.

Salespeople should be well-compensated, professional people who sit inside—ideally in one central location—and spend 8 hours a day, 5 days a week, engaged in selling conversations. That's 8 hours a day, 5 days a week, per person, engaged in the relentless pursuit of new business—new accounts and new categories for existing accounts.

That, ladies and gentlemen is how you're going to shift from single- to double-digit growth.

Replenish your salespeople's opportunity queues daily

But wait, wait, wait.

I know you've just seen the light. But, there's one more piece to this puzzle that needs to drop into place before your organization starts growing again.

It's true that double-digit growth will come from a small team of salespeople, dedicating 8 hours a day, 5 days a week, to the pursuit of new business. But that adds up to a lot of selling conversations. And for those selling conversations to occur, your salespeople will need a LOT of sales opportunities.

From where, you might ask, will these sales opportunities come?

It turns out that question is a little tricky to answer. It depends on your definition of "sales opportunity" (or what salespeople often call "leads").

Your sales team would like you to define a "sales opportunity" as a potential customer with both the means and the intent to purchase.

This highly limiting definition might have been excusable when your salespeople were busy looking after existing accounts.

But, if you sanction this definition, then I have bad news for you. You will NEVER be able to generate sales opportunities at the rate necessary to achieve double-digit growth.

However, if you define "sales opportunity" as simply a competitor's existing customer. Then you're in luck. Sales opportunities are abundant.

I would encourage you to mandate the second definition.

Now that you know what a sales opportunity is, all you need to do is assemble a bunch of them and maintain a queue of these opportunities upstream from each of your salespeople. And now your salespeople can busy themselves on the relentless pursuit of these opportunities.

The maintenance of salespeople's opportunity queues should be the responsibility of your Marketing department. My advice is to divide Marketing into two teams. You have your existing marketing-communications team, and then you have a small promotions team whose sole reason for existence is the daily replenishment of salespeople's opportunity queues.

LOOK WHAT YOU'VE DONE!

I think it's worth pausing here for a moment and reflecting on what you've achieved.

You've transferred the responsibility for revenue to your Operations group—which is to say that Operations is now responsible for what you used to call account management.

You've made Marketing responsible for the daily replenishment of salespeople's opportunity queues.

And you now have a small team of internal salespeople who dedicate themselves to the relentless pursuit of new business.

Relative to the organization you had prior to these changes, your customers are now enjoying a higher level of service AND you are pursuing new business at probably ten times your previous rate.

Bravo!

TWO LOOSE ENDS

But, before we're done here, there are two loose ends that need to be identified and neatly knotted.

Cold calling

The first is the subject of cold calling. You may already have realized that if you define a sales opportunity as a competitor's existing customer, then you are expecting your salespeople to pick up the phone and talk to strangers.

This is what salespeople call cold calling—and salespeople hate cold calling.

Well, I agree with salespeople on their dislike for cold calling. But I disagree on the definition.

What makes a telephone call COLD is not the absence of a pre-existing relationship; it's the absence of a compelling proposition. After all, if your salespeople took to regularly calling family and friends with Amway pitches, it wouldn't take long for those calls to turn a little chilly!

So, yes, your salespeople need to be prepared to talk to strangers. But, your senior executive team has to provide your salespeople with compelling propositions, so as to ensure that their selling conversations are reasonably productive.

And this brings us, full circle, back to Prince Castle and Xerox in the 50s.

It turns out that there are two kinds of compelling proposition. There's new technology, like Prince Castle's Multimixer. Or there's a service wrapper around existing technology like Xerox's pay-per-print proposition.

It's outside the scope of our little discussion here today to talk about HOW to generate a compelling proposition but if you don't have one, it should be a priority—and it must be the responsibility of your organization's most senior people.

What becomes of legacy salespeople

The second loose end is an uncomfortable question with a surprisingly comforting answer.

The question is, what will become of your existing salespeople?

Not surprisingly, few of them will be comfortable with the idea of surrendering their car keys, moving inside, and donning a headset.

Salespeople's discomfort with this idea should be shared by the executive team. After all, in most industrial organizations, salespeople have years of experience and technical knowledge that would be a huge loss to the organization, were it to walk out the door.

The key to resolving this dilemma is to recognize that your legacy salespeople are performing valuable roles today, as quasi-members of your Operations group. What you want to do is move your legacy salespeople into those roles, within Operations, that most closely resemble the actual activities they are performing today.

If some salespeople spend most of their time solving technical problems and designing solutions, make them members of your

Engineering team. If some salespeople enjoy managing the complexities associated with major accounts, make them Account Managers. And if you have salespeople who enjoy logistics, then maybe they should be the founding members of your new Onboarding team.

What many organizations do is create a hybrid role called "Field Specialist". These are semi-technical folks, with a decent understanding of commercials, who spend almost all of their time in the field, performing discreet tasks at the behest of both the sales and the customer service team.

Not surprisingly, many industrial salespeople find that this Field Specialist role enables them to enjoy the best elements of their previous sales role without the less-desirable elements and definitely without that sense of guilt as they drive home each day!

DOUBLE-DIGIT GROWTH

So, you now understand how to redesign your organization so you can comfortably generate double-digit growth, year after year.

The proximate cause of this growth will be your salespeople—who are now focused exclusively on the pursuit of new business.

But I think you understand now that this desirable end result cannot be achieved by edict alone.

It requires a new understanding of revenue.

It requires a recalibration of responsibilities across your Sales and Operational groups.

And—most importantly—it requires a purposeful and carefully orchestrated restructuring of your entire front-of-house.

The journey you're about to embark on is not easy. But it's necessary. It's overdue. And the upside is significant.

If you'd like to explore these ideas in greater detail, you might like to go to Amazon and grab a copy of my book. The Machine. And it probably wouldn't hurt to share this video with members of your executive team.

How about we agree—you and me—that last year will be the last year that you booked single-digit growth. Going forward, with your reengineered front-of-house. Double Digits.

Follow Justin

linkedin.com/in/justinroffmarsh
x.com/justinroffmarsh

About the Author

Justin Roff-Marsh is a management radical and an expert in the Theory of Constraints.

He's best known for his approach to sales, management and, consequently, rails against standard practices like salespeople's autonomous mode of operation, commission-based compensation, salespeople's ownership of accounts and much, much more!

In place of the traditional approach, he advocates that the sales function should be a 'machine', featuring the division of labor, the centralization of everything other than critical field visits and a formal approach to management.

After school, Justin rejected an offer from an engineering college and, instead, opted to study classical ballet full-time. While he loved ballet, he didn't care for the lifestyle of a dancer so he changed direction again.

He achieved immediate financial success as commissioned insurance salesperson then progressed rapidly to sales management. Before leaving the insurance industry he ran a team of 100 salespeople.

His next stop was a financial-services start-up and it was there that he developed his radical approach to sales. This approach contributed to the rapid growth of The Hudson Institute (Australia) which, in turn, prompted Justin to pine for his own business.

He founded Ballistix as a direct-marketing agency some 20 years ago and subsequently added consulting services. Today, Ballistix has clients in Australia, the United Kingdom and the United States of America. Justin emigrated to the USA in 2008 to lead Ballistix's growth there (and to hone his tennis game in the Californian sunshine!)

Made in the USA
Monee, IL
11 April 2025

15528173R00056